13 Colonies

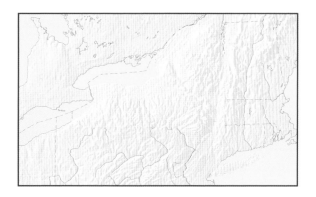

NEW YORK

13 Colonies

NEW YORK

The History of New York Colony, 1624–1776

ROBERTA WIENER AND JAMES R. ARNOLD

Chicago, Illinois

For information, address the publisher:
Raintree, 100 N. LaSalle, Suite 1200, Chicago, IL 60602

Printed in China by South China Printing.
09 08 07 06 05
10 9 8 7 6 5 4 3 2 1

Library of Congress Cataloging-in-Publication Data
Wiener, Roberta, 1952-
 New York / Roberta Wiener and James R. Arnold.
     p. cm. -- (13 colonies)
Summary: A detailed look at the formation of the colony of New York, its government, and its overall history, plus a prologue on world events in 1624 and an epilogue on New York today. Includes bibliographical references and index.
   ISBN 0-7398-6884-5 (lib. bdg.) -- ISBN 1-4109-0308-7 (pbk.)
   1. New York (State)--History--Colonial period, ca. 1600-1775--Juvenile
literature. 2. New York (State)--History--Revolution,
1775-1783--Juvenile literature. [1. New York (State)--History--Colonial
period, ca. 1600-1775. 2. New York (State)--History--Revolution,
1775-1783.] I. Arnold, James R. II. Title. III. Series: Wiener,
Roberta, 1952- 13 colonies.
   F122.W49 2004
   974.7'02--dc21
                                2003011059

Disclaimer
All the Internet addresses (URLs) given in this book were valid at the time of going to press. However, due to the dynamic nature of the Internet, some addresses may have changed, or sites may have changed or ceased to exist since publication. While the author and publishers regret any inconvenience this may cause readers, no responsibility for any such changes can be accepted by either the author or the publishers.

The paper used to print this book comes from sustainable resources.

Some words are shown in bold, **like this.** You can find out what they mean by looking in the glossary.

Title page picture: Lake Erie, which was named after the Erie Native Americans. A small part of its shoreline borders northwestern New York.

Opposite: New York City in 1763.

The authors wish to thank Walter Kossmann, whose knowledge, patience, and ability to ask all the right questions have made this a better series.

PICTURE ACKNOWLEDGMENTS

ARCHITECT OF THE CAPITOL: Cover, 11, 44 bottom, 57 bottom AUTHORS: 46, 59 ANNE S.K. BROWN MILITARY COLLECTION, BROWN UNIVERSITY LIBRARY, PROVIDENCE, RI: 38, 48 bottom, 57 top COLONIAL WILLIAMSBURG FOUNDATION: 5, 6, 12, 27, 34 top, 35 bottom right, 40 top, 52-53 J.G. HECK, *Iconographic Encyclopedia of Science, Literature, and Art*, 1851: 7 *Howard Pyle's Book of the American Spirit*, 1923: 24, 28, 43 INDEPENDENCE NATIONAL HISTORICAL PARK: 56 top LIBRARY OF CONGRESS: 8, 9, 10, 15, 16, 17, 20, 22-23, 25, 29, 30, 33, 34 bottom, 35 bottom left, 42, 44 top, 47, 48 top, 49, 51 bottom, 53, 55 NATIONAL ARCHIVES: 31, 32, 36-37, 51 top, 54, 58 bottom NATIONAL PARK SERVICE, COLONIAL NATIONAL HISTORICAL PARK: 26-27 COLLECTION OF THE NEW-YORK HISTORICAL SOCIETY: 21 (#1949.9), 41 (#1926.84) I. N. PHELPS STOKES COLLECTION, NEW YORK PUBLIC LIBRARY: Title page, 18-19, 40 bottom, 56 bottom COURTESY OF THE NORTH CAROLINA OFFICE OF ARCHIVES AND HISTORY: 50 PHILADELPHIA FREE LIBRARY: 35 top

CONTENTS

PROLOGUE: THE WORLD IN 1624

By 1624, the year the Dutch West India Company established New Netherland in North America, Europe had enjoyed more than 150 years of invention and discovery. The German invention of the printing press began the rapid spread of knowledge. The invention of better firearms changed the nature of war. Advances in navigation and the building of better sailing ships made longer voyages possible. So a new age of exploration dawned, with great seamen from Portugal, Spain, Italy, France, and England sailing into uncharted waters.

The world according to a European mapmaker around 1570

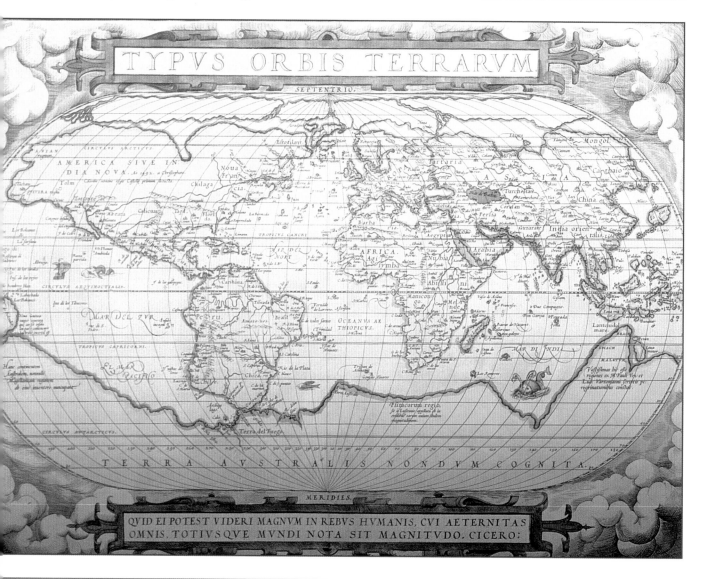

Not since the age of Viking exploration, some 500 years earlier, had European seamen sailed to unknown places. During the 1400s and 1500s, Portuguese sailors reached Africa, India, the Pacific Ocean, China, and Japan. They encountered kingdoms and civilizations that had existed for centuries. Everywhere, they found warlords struggling to expand their kingdoms.

A flock of birds flying during the age of exploration from Europe eastward over Asia would have first seen the Turks, who had conquered a huge empire that encompassed much of Eastern Europe, the Middle East, and North Africa. This flock would then have seen that the Russians had just conquered and annexed Siberia. Flying east, the flock would come to China. Here was a land of some 60 million people, long ruled from Beijing by the Ming dynasty. China was in decline but still looking for opportunities to conquer and expand. Conflict raged along China's borders, particularly with the Koreans and the Japanese. Continuing east, the flock

Europeans viewed the people of Japan as exotic and mysterious.

Dutch: the nationality of people born in the Netherlands

Netherlands: "low countries"; a European nation formed by the union of several low-lying provinces, including Holland. Amsterdam is the capital city.

New World: western hemisphere of the earth, including North America, Central America, and South America; so-called because the people of the Old World, in the east, did not know about the existence of the Americas until the 1400s

would have crossed the water to Japan. Japan was recently unified under a single conqueror and had begun trading with Europeans for the first time. For a short while, **Dutch** traders were the only Europeans permitted to trade with Japan.

Had the flock then made a u-turn over the Pacific Ocean and flown back west, they would have seen India. India was a great land of 100 million people, recently united under the rule of the conqueror, Akbar the Great. Turning to the southwest, they would have found Africa. On the African coasts were small kingdoms and several great empires, often at war and often changing leadership. The interior of Africa remained unknown to outsiders.

Europeans did not yet have a clear idea where all these lands were located. But the Portuguese and other Europeans knew enough to see great opportunities. They saw the chance to grow rich from trade in exotic spices. They saw souls ready to be converted to Christianity. They saw the chance to make conquests of their own and expand their countries into great empires. And not least, they saw the dark-skinned people of Africa and, thinking them a different species, they saw the chance to capture and sell slaves. Traders from the **Netherlands** began joining other Europeans in voyaging to Africa, Asia, and the Pacific to trade in spices and slaves. They eventually formed the Dutch East India Company.

Thousands of African slaves were brought across the Atlantic Ocean by European traders. The captives were chained and packed tightly into ships, so that the slave traders would have more people to sell at the end of the voyage. Many captives died on the ships from disease, cold, and starvation.

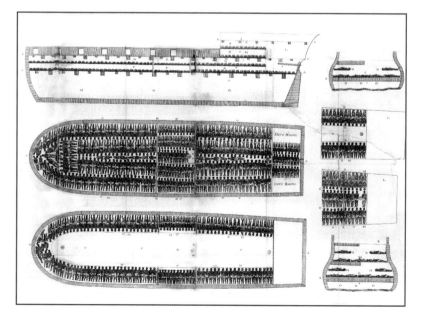

The voyages from Europe to these distant shores were long and dangerous. Explorers had to sail from Europe all the way around Africa. So, European explorers began to search for a shortcut. They believed a northwest passage lay somewhere to the west, and a northeast passage through the Arctic ice to the northeast. In 1492, Christopher Columbus landed on an island on the far side of the Atlantic Ocean and claimed it for Spain. He thought that he had actually sailed straight around the world and come to an island near India. Years of exploration by numerous sailors would pass before the people of Europe realized that Columbus had been the first European of their era to set foot in a land unknown to them. They called this land the **New World**, although it was not new to the people who lived there.

After Columbus, Amerigo Vespucci claimed to have reached the New World. Whether he actually did or not, a mapmaker put his name on a map in 1507, and the New World became **America**, or the Americas. Still looking for that shortcut to the riches of Asia, explorers from Spain, France, and England continued to sail to North and South America. They began to claim large pieces of these lands for their own nations. Giovanni da Verrazano, an Italian employed by the king of France, was the first European to explore the coast of present-day New York in 1524.

In 1607 England planted its first, barely successful, North American **colony** at Jamestown, Virginia. One of the colony's founders, Captain John Smith, sailed along the coast and up the rivers hoping he would be the one to find the Northwest Passage. Not to be outdone by the exploring sea captains of her rivals, the Netherlands joined the search for a passage to Asia when the Dutch East India Company hired the English captain, Henry Hudson. In 1609 Hudson sailed up the American river that would later bear his name. Failing to find the Northwest Passage, he turned back at the site of present-day Albany, New York.

While Hudson explored under Dutch sponsorship, Samuel de Champlain, who founded the capital of New France at Quebec in 1608, entered present-day New York from the north and defeated a group of Mohawk North Americans at the lake now called Lake Champlain. The French established a fort on the lake and traded with the **Native Americans**. This fort would play a part in later

AMERICA: LAND THAT CONTAINS THE CONTINENTS OF NORTH AMERICA AND SOUTH AMERICA

Giovanni da Verrazano, the first European to explore the coast of New York has a bridge in New York City named after him.

COLONY: LAND OWNED AND CONTROLLED BY A DISTANT NATION; A COLONIST IS A PERMANENT SETTLER OF A COLONY

battles between the French and the English. In 1620 English people had first started a colony on the coast of New England. So it was that, in the opening years of the 17th century, citizens of three powerful European nations gathered around what would one day prove to be an important part of the world.

Henry Hudson's ship, the *Half Moon*, leaves Amsterdam on a voyage of exploration.

The Fate of Henry Hudson

When Henry Hudson and his crew of English and Dutch sailors set out in the Half Moon in 1609, they were working for the Dutch East India Company. Hudson had sailed twice before to the Arctic to find a northeast passage, a way through the ice north of Siberia to Asia. On those voyages he was employed by London merchants.

On his third voyage, Hudson searched again for a northeast passage, but failed to find one. He had promised his Dutch employers that he would return to the Netherlands after exploring the Arctic. Instead he sailed the Half Moon across the Atlantic Ocean to Maine. From Maine, Hudson and his crew searched for a northwest passage in Chesapeake Bay, Delaware Bay, and then the Hudson River, trading with the Native Americans for furs as they went. The Half Moon sailed about 150 miles up the Hudson, as far as a large ship could go.

Hudson was unable to maintain discipline or exert authority over his men, and they came close to mutiny several times. A last threat of mutiny cut short Hudson's voyage, and he returned across the Atlantic as his men demanded. When the ship reached England, authorities there would not let Hudson and the English sailors in his crew go on to the Netherlands. However, Hudson was able to send his log detailing his discoveries to the Netherlands.

In 1610, English merchants hired Hudson to make another voyage to America, to again search for the northwest passage. On this voyage, on the ship Discovery, Hudson explored the frigid northern bay, now part of Canada, which would eventually be named after him. After a brutal winter in northern Canada, Hudson's inability to control his crew proved fatal. In June 1611, the men mutinied. They set Hudson, his son, and

seven other men adrift in a small rowboat. That is the last anyone on record ever saw of Henry Hudson. Only a handful of the mutineers were on the ship when it finally reached England. A number of men, including the mutiny's ringleaders, had been killed in a battle with Inuit.

More than 20 years later, another explorer found the remnants of a shack on Hudson Bay that may have been built by the abandoned Hudson and his companions. In 1670 English merchants formed the Hudson's Bay Company, to continue the search for a northwest passage and to conduct trade in Canada.

Hudson met and traded with Native Americans as he explored the Hudson River.

I.
THE DUTCH WEST INDIA COMPANY

Traders from the Netherlands had formed the Dutch East India Company in 1602 to trade with the people of Asia and the South Pacific. In 1614 the Dutch East India Company built a trading post, called Fort Nassau, on an island in the Hudson River near the site of present-day Albany, New York. Discouraged by flooding, they abandoned the post. Not until ten years later would they build another one, this time on the drier riverbank.

A merchant's office in the Netherlands. A group of Dutch merchants formed the Dutch West India Company.

Soon Dutch traders saw the need for another trading company, to take advantage of the money-making opportunities of the Americas. The Dutch already had trading posts on islands in the warm waters of the Caribbean Sea. Since Europeans had once believed that the islands off the coast of America were just to the west of India, they called these islands the West Indies. The Dutch called their new trading company, organized in 1621, the Dutch West India Company.

At this time the Netherlands was at war, fighting for independence from Spain. The Netherlands' fight with Spain was part of a wider European war called the Thirty Years'

War, which lasted from 1618 to 1648. The Dutch hoped to use their new American post as a base for raiding Spain's American colonies.

In 1624 a group of Dutch traders led by Cornelius May settled at the Netherlands' Hudson riverside post, formerly Fort Nassau, now called Fort Orange. About thirty families came to live there. Fort Orange became the first permanent European settlement in what would become New York. Its central location at the crossroads of the routes between New England, New France, and Iroquois country turned it into a meeting place. There the Dutch offered the Native Americans metal tools, beads, cloth, guns, and ammunition in exchange for furs. A few Dutch traders settled at another post, also named Fort Nassau, on the Delaware River, and another handful settled at the mouth of the Hudson River.

2.
NEW YORK IN 1624

The land that would become New York once was nearly flat. But many thousands of years ago, glaciers spread over most of the land, carving out valleys and leaving behind thousands of lakes. New York became a land of highlands and lowlands, mountains and plains, surrounded and divided by major waterways.

New York's highland regions are the Appalachian Highlands, the Adirondack Upland, and the New England Upland. New York's highest mountain peak, Mount Marcy, stands 5,344 feet (1,630 meters) above sea level. Fertile lowland regions surround Lake Ontario, Lake Erie,

❶ St. Lawrence Lowland
❷ Adirondack Upland
❸ Great Lakes Lowland
❹ Appalachian Highlands
❺ Hudson-Mohawk Lowland
❻ New England Upland
❼ Atlantic Coastal Plain

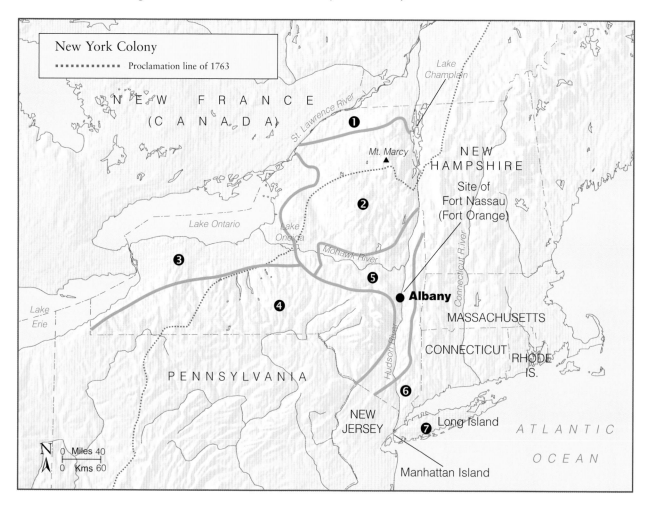

and the St. Lawrence, Mohawk, and Hudson Rivers. The Atlantic coastal plain region includes Long Island and a part of present-day New York City. New York City benefits from one of the world's great natural harbors. The climate varies with the landscape. Northern and western New York endure colder winters and enormous snowfalls, but enjoy cooler summers than the rest of the state.

The Iroquois people lived in the Mohawk Valley's upper and central parts as well as in the lake region of central New York. Their name came from the distinctive structures they built, and translates as "People of the

In 1609 Samuel de Champlain led French troops in an attack on an Iroquois village, a group of bark-covered longhouses surrounded by a wall of logs. Longhouses ranged from 40 to more than 300 feet (12 to 91 meters) in length and were occupied by several families. Iroquois lived in longhouses until the late 1700s.

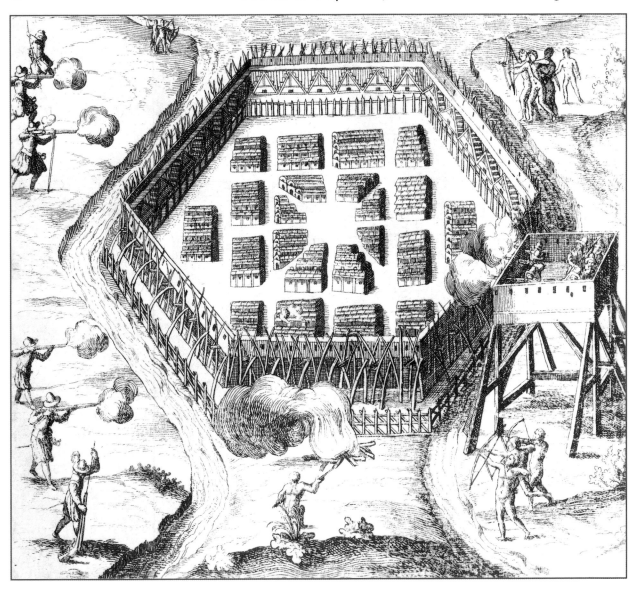

An Iroquois woman, drawn at the time Champlain explored Iroquois country. Women had political power in the Iroquois League. Historians estimate that the Iroquois League formed some time between 1570 and 1600.

longhouse." In fact, most Iroquois lived in communities of bark-covered longhouses that had doors at each end rather than at their sides. Larger villages had from 30 to 150 longhouses. Often a fortified wall built from large logs surrounded the villages.

The Iroquois were an aggressive warrior people. In times past, the five main Iroquois groups had fought among themselves. Some remarkable leaders, including most notably Hiawatha, made peace among the Iroquoian-speaking Seneca, Oneida, Onondaga, Mohawk, and Cayuga. This peace led to the famous Iroquois League.

The Iroquois League was a very sophisticated form of governmental organization. The League relied upon its members agreeing as a group; in other words, the members of the league reached a consensus. The consensus came by observing a ritual. Senior clanswomen selected special men and appointed them sachems. The sachems met at the council fire at Onondaga to discuss policy. The most successful sachems worked hard to make sure all members agreed. The result was unity among the members of the League. This unity gave the Iroquois League enormous political and economic power.

The Five Nations tried to take weaker Native American nations under their protection as allies or dependents. The Five Nations treated those who refused as enemies. Trade with the Dutch gave the Iroquois guns and this gave them a dominant advantage in war with other Native American groups. The Iroquois became the most feared warriors in eastern North America. They expanded to dominate an area from Maine to the Mississippi River, as far south as the Cumberland River of Tennessee. There were about 5,500 Iroquois in 1600. The expansion of their empire led to an increase to about 16,000 in 1689.

Besides the Iroquois, other groups of Native Americans lived in New York. Among them were the Erie, who lived in the west along the shore of the great lake named after them. Algonquian-speaking Delaware Indians also lived in parts of New York including the island of Manhattan.

LONGHOUSE: A LONG STRUCTURE WITH A ROUNDED ROOF, MADE OF BENT SAPLINGS COVERED WITH BARK, AND DIVIDED INTO ROOMS BY PARTITIONS.

An Iroquois man at about the time Europeans first encountered the Iroquois.

MAHICAN / MOHEGAN / MOHICAN: THREE DIFFERENT WAYS OF SPELLING THE NAME OF THE ALGONQUIAN-SPEAKING HUDSON VALLEY NATIVE AMERICANS WHO COMPETED UNSUCCESSFULLY FOR LAND AND TRADE WITH THEIR MOHAWK RIVALS

WAMPUM: ALGONQUIAN WORD FOR BEADS MADE OF SHELLS AND USED AS MONEY

Two other Algonquian-speaking groups in New York were the Montauks and the **Mahicans**.

The Montauks lived on the eastern part of what is today called Long Island. Possibly 5,000 Native American people belonging to several closely related groups lived in this area during the early 1600s. The Montauks made beads out of seashells, and these beads—called "**wampum**"—were used for money and trade, and were important to Native American life throughout New York and neighboring colonies.

The Mahicans lived in the upper Hudson River valley. About 5,000 Mahicans lived in walled towns. The log walls protected them against raids from the neighboring Mohawks, who were trying to gain control of the fur trade with Europeans. The Mohawks, members of the Iroquois League, forced the Mahicans to move their towns away from the Dutch trading posts. Then the Dutch purchased land from the Mahicans in order to build more trading posts and settlements.

Lake Erie, which was named after the Erie Native americans. A small part of its shoreline borders northwestern New York.

3.
THE DUTCH IN AMERICA

The year 1624 marked the official beginning of New Netherland, the Netherlands' North American colony. Dutch **merchants** were the first Europeans to settle an area extending from the Connecticut River to the Delaware River. The following year, more Dutch settlers came to Manhattan Island. They called the settlement New Amsterdam, and built a fort, a church, and a house for the colony's governor, who had the title Director General. In 1626 the director general purchased Manhattan Island from the Native Americans for the equivalent of $24 worth of wampum and other trade goods. Eventually, the Dutch tried to control Connecticut, New Jersey, and Delaware as well as New York.

The 1626 purchase of Manhattan by Peter Minuit for $24 became a legend more than two centuries after it supposedly occurred. The only known facts about this purchase are: a New Netherland official purchased Manhattan from the Native Americans during the early days of the colony; and another Dutch official wrote a letter in 1626 stating that the payment consisted of merchandise valued at about 60 guilders (Dutch money).

INDENTURED SERVANT: PERSON WHO AGREED TO WORK AS A SERVANT FOR A CERTAIN NUMBER OF YEARS IN EXCHANGE FOR FOOD, CLOTHING, A PLACE TO SLEEP, AND PAYMENT OF ONE'S PASSAGE ACROSS THE ATLANTIC TO THE COLONIES

MERCHANT: TRADER; PERSON WHO BUYS AND RE-SELLS MERCHANDISE

Unlike other Europeans who came to America to escape poverty or religious persecution, the main Dutch interest in the colony was trade. Few Dutch people wanted to leave the Netherlands permanently to live in America. Traders who came to New Netherland wanted to make money and then return home.

Some of the early Dutch settlers of New Netherland were **indentured servants** who worked for the Dutch West India Company. After they served for about six years, they were rewarded with land, tools, livestock, and seeds with

A farm in the Bronx, now a crowded part of modern-day New York City. The name Bronx came from the name of an early settler, Jonas Bronck. Yonkers, just up the Hudson River from the Bronx, received its name from a Dutch settler who had the formal title, *jonker* which means "young gentleman."

PATROON: DUTCH WORD FOR "PROTECTOR", A PERSON WHO RECEIVED OWNERSHIP RIGHTS OVER A LARGE ESTATE IN RETURN FOR BRINGING COLONISTS TO NEW NETHERLAND

which to start their lives as freemen. The fertile land of Manhattan Island was good for growing grain, and the settlers were able to support themselves as farmers. However, they were required to sell all their produce to the company and buy all their supplies from the company. The company also insisted on controlling all the fur trade. By the time the colony was five years old, only 300 people had chosen to settle there, with perhaps ten African slaves.

In an effort to attract more settlers, the directors of the Dutch West India Company offered its investors a special deal. If an investor paid to bring at least 50 workers to New Netherland, he was permitted to buy a huge piece of land from the Native Americans. He then had the authority to govern the land and collect rent from the people who farmed it. The Dutch called such an estate a **patroonship** and its owner the patroon (Dutch word for protector). The patroon was also supposed to pay for a minister and schoolteacher for his estate. Killaen van

New Amsterdam in 1643. New Amsterdam, on the tip of Manhattan Island, eventually grew to become New York City, one of the world's great cities.

MONOPOLY: EXCLUSIVE RIGHT TO CONTROL THE PURCHASE AND SALE OF SPECIFIC GOODS OR SERVICES

PROTESTANT: MEMBER OF ANY CHRISTIAN CHURCH THAT HAS BROKEN AWAY FROM ROMAN CATHOLIC OR EASTERN ORTHODOX CONTROL

PURITANS: PROTESTANTS WHO WANTED THE CHURCH OF ENGLAND TO PRACTICE A MORE "PURE" FORM OF CHRISTIANITY, AND ESTABLISHED A COLONY IN NEW ENGLAND

Rensselaer, a major investor in the Dutch West India Company, bought a large piece of land near Fort Orange from the Mahicans. On it he established one of the earliest patroonships, called Rensselaerswyk. He settled more than 200 people there to farm the land.

Gradually, the company gave up its **monopoly** on all trade in the colony. This attracted a greater number of settlers. By 1660 about 5,000 Europeans with about 600 African slaves lived in New Netherland. Like the home country, New Netherland tolerated people of various religions. The Dutch Reformed church was favored, however. The authorities believed that welcoming all sorts of people was good for the colony and good for business. As a result, Jews and **Protestants** from other European countries such as Belgium and France settled in New Netherland. New Englanders fleeing the religious intolerance of the **Puritans** also found New Netherland attractive.

At first, the Dutch took great care to avoid conflict with the Native Americans. They purchased all the land on which the traders and colonists settled, and refused to

be drawn into the trade rivalry between the Algonquian-speaking Mahicans and the Iroquoian Mohawks. But when the Mohawks decisively defeated the Mahicans in 1628, the West India Company formally recognized the Mohawks as their trading partners.

As the town of New Amsterdam grew, the colonists and the neighboring Algonquians came into increasing conflict. Settlers' cattle and hogs trampled and ate the

A slave auction. The Dutch imported slaves from Africa and the West Indies. As time went on, slavery grew less prevalent in New York. A visitor wrote, "Many people cannot conquer the idea of its being contrary to the laws of Christianity to keep slaves." Many New Yorkers set their slaves free, and some freed slaves went to live among the Native Americans. By 1772, only 23 slaves were imported to New York, in contrast to 7,200 imported into South Carolina. That same year, no slaves were imported into Pennsylvania, and only eight to all of New England.

Native Americans' cornfields, so the Native Americans killed and ate the livestock, which angered the settlers. The director general, Willem Kieft, ordered the Native Americans to pay rents and taxes to the colonial government, but the native people refused to recognize an outsider's authority over them.

When Native Americans killed two colonists in an argument, Kieft demanded that the suspects be turned

Europeans called the Native Americans savages, but demonstrated their own savagery by killing defenseless Native American men, women, and children. By 1670 an English government official on Long Island observed, with great satisfaction: "To say something of the Indians, there is now but few upon the Island, and those few no ways hurtful but rather serviceable to the English, and it is to be admired, how strangely they have decreased by the hand of God, since the English first settling of those parts; for since my time, where there were six towns, they are reduced to two small villages, and it hath been generally observed, that where the English come to settle, a divine hand makes way for them, by removing or cutting off the Indians either by wars one with the other, or by some raging mortal Disease."

over to the colonial authorities for punishment. The Native Americans refused, and Kieft decided to take revenge on an entire village, one that had nothing to do with the killings. On February 25, 1643, Dutch troops burned a village full of some 80 defenseless Algonquian refugees who had fled the Mohawks. As the Native Americans fled, the soldiers killed them all, even women and children. Two years of bloodshed followed, a cycle of Native American attacks on colonial farms and settlements answered by colonial massacres of entire Native American villages. One such massacre, led by a hired New England officer locally famous for slaughtering Native Americans, eliminated more than 500 Native Americans. This period of war ended with at least 1,000 Native Americans slaughtered and colonial settlements in smoking ruin.

Between 1655 and 1664, the Dutch colonists went to war with the Algonquians three more times. One of these wars was called the Peach War, because it began with the murder of a Native American woman as she took peaches from a colonist's trees. In the end, the Algonquians lost most of their land around New Amsterdam, but potential settlers feared to move there because of the nearly constant fighting. Those who did

Right: A major source of filth in the streets of New Amsterdam was the chamber pot, which served as a toilet. Townspeople emptied them into the streets. Not until the early 1700s did New York begin building underground sewers beneath the city streets, so that residents could pour their waste into the sewers instead of simply dumping it into the gutters.

Left: One notable victim of the ongoing warfare between settlers and Indians was Anne Hutchinson. Hutchinson and her family were killed by Native Americans on Long Island in 1644. She had been expelled from Puritan New England for her religious beliefs.

A pamphlet published in old Amsterdam described life in New Amsterdam: "Everyone there who fills no public office is busy about his own affairs. Men work there as in **Holland** [the largest province of the Netherlands]; one trades...; another builds houses; the third farms. Each farmer has his farmstead ..."

> HOLLAND: MAIN PROVINCE OF THE NETHERLANDS, OFTEN USED INCORRECTLY TO REFER TO THE NETHERLANDS

settle in New Amsterdam, only about 1,300 by 1660, lived in a dirty town with hogs and other animals wandering the streets to eat the plentiful garbage left by the residents.

Warfare with the Native Americans was not the only thing that kept potential colonists from choosing New Netherland. The colony's governors did not let the colonists have much say in the colonial government. On a few occasions, a director general allowed the colonists to send representatives to meet with him. In every case, the director became annoyed by the representatives' demands and sent them away. Peter Stuyvesant was director general from 1646 until New Netherland fell to England in 1664. A soldier and former governor of a Dutch colony in the Caribbean, Stuyvesant made all the laws, chose all public officials, and imposed whatever taxes he saw fit. Naturally, not everyone was pleased with his decisions. A group of colonists complained to the Dutch West India

Company in 1650, accusing Stuyvesant of corruption: "There scarcely comes a ship in or near here, which, if it does not belong to friends, is not regarded as a prize by him … confiscating has reached such a pitch in New Netherland that nobody who has any visible property considers it to be at all safe."

Peter Stuyvesant made a treaty with the New England authorities to set the boundary between New England and New Netherland in 1650. Concerned about the Swedish colony to the south, in present-day Delaware, he ordered a fort to be built near the capital of New Sweden. When New Sweden's governor captured the fort, Stuyvesant recaptured it and forced the governor to surrender the entire colony to New Netherland in 1655.

Above: Peter Stuyvesant held almost absolute power in the colony of New Netherland, but had to humble himself before the authorities in the Netherlands. For example, he wrote to the government in the Netherlands, "I dare not interrupt your Illustrious High Mightiness' most important business. …" Such language was common among colonial officials addressing their superiors in Europe.

Left: Stuyvesant established Fort Casimir in New Sweden in 1651. When the Swedes captured it in 1654, they changed the name to Fort Trinity. The Swedes' action gave Stuyvesant the excuse he needed to take over the entire New Sweden colony.

4.
THE COMING OF THE ENGLISH

England had taken the Netherlands' side in the Thirty Years' War, but that war had ended in 1648. Soon, England and the Netherlands began to view one another as competitors for American trade goods. Their rivalry erupted into war on three separate occasions. England decided to expel the Dutch from New Netherland because its location between New England and Maryland prevented either from expanding, and because the Dutch

At first, Peter Stuyvesant angrily refused to surrender New Netherland to the English. He was so fond of New Amsterdam, however, that he chose to stay there and end his days under English rule. His farm was near the present-day intersection of Second Avenue and Tenth Street in New York City.

The Dutch settlers of New Netherland felt they had not received enough attention and help from the Netherlands. After the surrender of New Netherland, the New Amsterdam town council reported it to the directors of the Dutch West India Company, writing, "We, your Honors' loyal, sorrowful and desolate subjects, cannot … keep from relating the event, which … unexpectedly happened to us in consequence of your Honors' neglect and forgetfulness…." Below, Stuyvesant leads Dutch soldiers as they march out of New Amsterdam to formally surrender to the English.

competed with the English colonies for trade. During one of the Anglo-Dutch wars, a fleet of English ships sailed into New Amsterdam's harbor and demanded Peter Stuyvesant's surrender. The English fleet was too strong to resist, so Stuyvesant had to give in without a fight. He surrendered on August 27, 1664, and New Netherland became New York, named for the king's brother, the Duke of York. So certain were the English of victory that King Charles II had already given the duke a **charter** for the territory of New York on March 12, 1664.

Being badly outnumbered, Stuyvesant had not tried to resist, so the English gave the Dutch generous terms of surrender. The Dutch settlers could choose to stay or leave, they were permitted to keep their property, and new settlers from the Netherlands would be permitted to settle in New York. The Dutch people remaining in New York also retained their freedom of religion. The colonial government planned to collect taxes for support of churches, but each community could decide which church to support. Peter Stuyvesant himself lived out the rest of his life on his New York farm.

The Dutch Reformed church had been the dominant form of Protestantism in New Netherland, and its members continued to hold services after New Netherland became New York.

Richard Nicholls, the English commander of the expedition to take New Netherland, became governor and organized the government of New York to resemble that of the other English colonies. Citizens gained the right to elect some public officials. However, the colony did not gain an assembly, because Nicholls feared that too many Dutch representatives would be elected. The governor refused to appoint any Dutch colonists to his council. Nicholls changed the name of the town of New Amsterdam to New York, and Fort Orange became Fort Albany.

In 1672 another war erupted between England and the Netherlands. A strong Dutch fleet sailed into New York harbor in 1673 and forced the English governor to surrender without a fight, just as the English had done to Peter Stuyvesant. A year later, however, the Netherlands and England signed a treaty that returned the Netherlands' North American possessions to England for good.

A new governor, Edmund Andros, gave special trading privileges to the merchants of the city of New York. For example, they had a monopoly on producing flour for export. They paid fees to the government in return for

French Protestants, known as Huguenots, founded settlements in New Netherland and New York.

these privileges. Merchants in the rest of the colony complained bitterly. The colonists also complained about the lack of an elected assembly to represent them.

Finally, King James II (the former Duke of York who took the throne in 1685) ordered that Andros be replaced as governor. The king gave New York the right to elect an assembly. New York's first colonial assembly met in 1683, with both Dutch and English members. The assembly passed a set of laws, called the Charter of Liberties, granting equal rights to colonists of both nationalities. The king, however, decided that the charter was a dangerous document that gave the assembly too much power, so in 1686 he refused to approve it and disbanded the assembly.

James II was unpopular both in England and in the colonies, because he was Catholic and because he wanted more power. In 1688 the king earned the disapproval of New Yorkers when he decided to merge New York with the New England colonies, with the hated Edmund Andros as governor.

Kings and Queens

King James II ruled for barely three years, from 1685 to 1688. He was a Catholic, which many English people found objectionable, and he tried to bypass Parliament in making laws. Worse, he raised taxes throughout England's empire and tried to increase royal authority over the colonies. He banned the colonial legislatures and set a dictator, Sir Edmund Andros, over all of the New England colonies, plus New York and New Jersey. Andros began to collect rents from land that colonists already owned. Discontented Protestants in England wrote to James' Protestant nephew, William of Orange, in the Netherlands. William was married to James's daughter, Mary, also a Protestant. William landed in England with an army, and James fled to France, leaving the throne to William and Mary. Since William was Dutch, New York's Dutch population rejoiced when the news reached America, and hoped that Dutch rule over New York would be restored. King William III ruled England from 1689 to 1702, Queen Mary having died in 1694. Mary's sister Anne, also a Protestant, became queen in 1702. Queen Anne ruled until her death in 1714. Anne had been pregnant 18 times in her life, but only one child survived. When her son died, it was agreed that the succession to the throne would pass from Anne to another royal family. The next ruler of England, now part of Great Britain, was George Ludwig of Hanover, a German Lutheran great-grandson of King James I. He became King George I.

One of England's wars with France was called Queen Anne's War. England's union with Scotland and the formation of Great Britain also took place during the reign of Queen Anne.

After James II fled to France, Parliament offered the crown of England to William and Mary.

Soon thereafter, the people of New York began to hear rumors that had trickled south from New England. James II was no longer king, and had been driven from England and replaced by a Dutchman! The New England colonies had rebelled and overthrown Edmund Andros! Emboldened by the rumors, several English and Dutch towns overthrew their public officials and elected new officials to replace them. Then Jacob Leisler, a Dutch **militia** captain, quickly took control of New York and declared a new government in the form of a Committee of Safety, made up of representatives from the counties. The committee pledged loyalty to King William III and Queen Mary II, the Protestants who had replaced James II.

Leisler proved unable to govern New York. The English, not surprisingly, refused to support him. Leisler did not come from a wealthy family, so he gathered no support from wealthy Dutch New Yorkers either. Meanwhile, King William III sent a new governor, Colonel Henry Sloughter, to take over New York. When Sloughter arrived in 1691, Leisler delayed turning over power to

Above: A Hudson River mansion belonging to a wealthy Dutch family. Prosperous Dutch merchants remained influential in the colony after the English takeover.

Above: The famous blue and white Delft china from the Netherlands was much desired by both Dutch and English colonists.

Left: A New York farmhouse

him. Sloughter accused Leisler of treason and had him executed. Sloughter died later the same year, having lived just long enough to restore an effective government.

The next governor, Benjamin Fletcher, granted huge plots of land to the wealthiest colonists. These large land holdings were run according to the manorial system, long prevalent in Europe. Under the manorial system, the lord of the **manor** collected rent from **tenants** who farmed small plots. As a result, three quarters of New York farmers worked the land as tenants of about thirty owners of vast estates. Among the largest landowners were the Van Rensselaer, Livingston, Stuyvesant, Bayard, and Philips families. Men from such families also held most of the political offices. Several of New York's subsequent governors tried to gain popularity by making huge land grants to wealthy families. They also used their position of power to enrich themselves by collecting bribes and stealing from the colonial treasury.

Relatively little land remained for average people to buy, so few New Yorkers could realize the dream of owning a family farm. Still, people moved to New York, and most settled along the Hudson River Valley, south of Albany. Farther north, the presence of the Iroquois and the prospect of war with the French discouraged English settlement.

THE FRENCH FRONTIER

England and France were great rivals who, throughout their history, had often resorted to war to resolve disagreements. Even during peaceful times they competed fiercely. When **British** and French settlers came to North America, they brought their conflict with them. New France lay to the north of New York, in present-day Canada. However, Iroquois country was located between the English and French colonies, and the Iroquois had allied themselves with the English. Many other Native Americans became allies of the French.

As the 1600s drew to a close, the French in North America and their Native American allies grew in numbers and strength. New Yorkers began to fear that the French would attack them by traveling down Lake Champlain and the Hudson River into the heart of their colony. They

BRITISH: NATIONALITY OF A PERSON BORN IN GREAT BRITAIN. PEOPLE BORN IN ENGLAND ARE CALLED "ENGLISH"

The French explorer LaSalle visited the Niagara Falls region on the border between New York and New France. Such explorations fed the ongoing conflict between the French and English in America.

worried that Catholic missionaries from France would convert the Native Americans and stir them up to fight a religious war.

Meanwhile, in 1688 England and France went to war with one another in Europe. The war continued until 1697, as they fought over territory in Europe as well as France's efforts to return James II to the throne of England. This war, and another war that raged from 1702 to 1713, spilled over into the American colonies. Throughout those years, French and Native American forces attacked the New York settlements, and New York's Native American allies attacked French settlements in a never-ending cycle of attacks and revenge. English colonists in New York and New England planned three different invasions of Canada but were never able to muster an effective force.

When war ended in Europe in 1713, the French gave up Newfoundland and Nova Scotia to the British, which made the border with Canada more secure for some New England colonists. New Yorkers still had the Iroquois country as a buffer between the British and the French. The Iroquois tried to appear neutral and get along with both colonial powers, so they could trade with both and not be forced to choose sides.

Wars in Europe spilled over into the colonies held by the warring European powers. From 1688 to 1697, England and the Netherlands fought France. This war was called the War of the Grand Alliance or the Nine Years' War in Europe. In America it was called King William's War, and battles took place in New York, New England, and Canada. From 1701 to 1714, Great Britain fought France and Spain in the War of the Spanish Succession, which in America was called Queen Anne's War and was fought in Canada, New England, and South Carolina. From 1740 to 1748, Britain fought Spain, France, and other European powers in the War of the Austrian Succession. In America, fighting began in 1744, and the conflict was called King George's War, with battles in Nova Scotia and New England. In America it was called the French and Indian War. Battles took place from Pennsylvania to Canada. In America, British troops were exposed for the first time to wilderness fighting from the cover of woods. In Europe the soldiers of the Seven Years' War fought in much more open terrain. Below, a battle in Europe in 1757.

THE GOLDEN AGE OF THE IROQUOIS LEAGUE

As European settlers moved inland to occupy more and more land, the settlers brought diseases that killed thousands of Native Americans. The diseases left the native nations weak. In New York, the Native American rivals to the Iroquois became so weak that the Iroquois were able to expand to control the lands where once these rivals had lived. Iroquois diplomats also cleverly took advantage of the ambitions of their Native American rivals and of the European settlers. They played one against the other and so increased their own power.

The period from 1701·to 1755 was the time when the Iroquois League enjoyed its greatest power. It was the Iroquois "golden age," a time of peace and prosperity. In 1700 the Iroquois League had about 10,000 members.

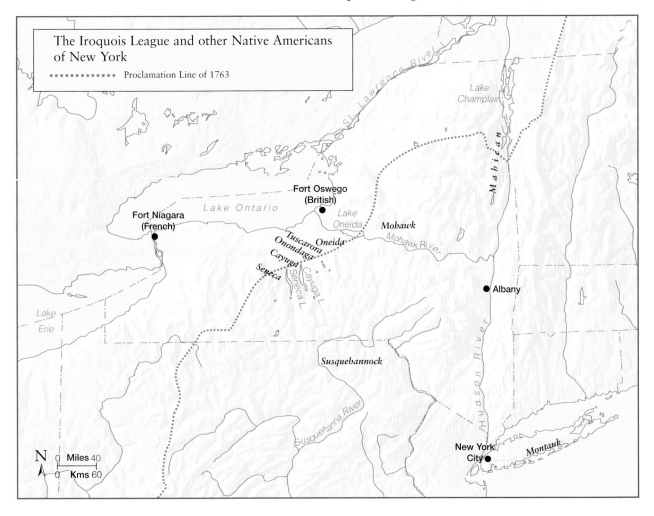

The Iroquois League and other Native Americans of New York

•••••••••••• Proclamation Line of 1763

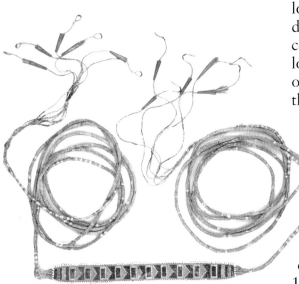

Native Americans in New York used halters such as this to secure their prisoners on the march. After a battle, the Iroquois often brought captives back to their villages and adopted them into their tribes.

Long Island as an artist saw it around the time of the Revolution.

The Iroquois thought of their league as if it were a longhouse. The Mohawks protected the building's eastern door. The Onondaga, who lived in the center of the confederacy, maintained the fire in the middle of the longhouse. The Oneida guarded the south and east sides of the longhouse while the Seneca and Cayuga watched the house's western door.

Iroquois leaders made a plan to stop white expansion into their territory. First and foremost, the Iroquois acted as a unified nation. Second, the Mohawks, who lived closest to the British, refused to sell very much land to British settlers. Third, the Iroquois took steps to increase their numbers. The Cayuga and Oneida took in Native Americans who had fled from white pressure. The Seneca adopted entire Native American communities from areas the Iroquois had conquered. In 1722, the League admitted the Tuscarora, a people whom the British had driven from their homes in North Carolina, as a sixth member nation.

During the Iroquois golden age, Iroquois hunters, trappers, and traders traveled throughout the northeast. Leaders managed to hold the League together and to block white expansion onto their lands. They controlled trade between Native Americans and Europeans across a wide region. But, there were about 250,000 white settlers who lived along the border of the Iroquois League, in New York and Pennsylvania. The settlers flowed into the Susquehanna Valley in these colonies, and this movement placed new pressure on the boundaries of the Iroquois nations.

In 1720 the Iroquois League let the French build a fort within their territory at Niagara. Then in 1727, in trying to get along with both Britain and France, they had to allow the British to build a fort at Oswego, also in Iroquois territory. Little by little, the Iroquois League was losing control of its territory.

The **frontier** trading forts became diplomatic centers, where the British and French negotiated with the Native Americans about trade and alliances.

Meanwhile, on Long Island, the Montauks struggled to survive as British neighbors settled around them. Some stayed on their ancestral lands and barely made a living by farming, fishing, whaling, or laboring for British employers. During the early 1700s, most moved to reservations, Christian missionary towns, or neighboring colonies. The Mahicans of the Hudson Valley had been reduced to fewer than 500 by epidemics, warfare, and migration. The survivors sold most of their land to European colonists and moved far away.

FRONTIER: NEWEST PLACE OF SETTLEMENT, LOCATED THE FARTHEST AWAY FROM THE CENTER OF POPULATION

THE GROWING COLONY

So much land had been taken up by the huge estates of the wealthy that colonial New York was not the first choice for immigrants hoping to own farms. A few German Protestants fleeing war in their homeland came to New York in 1710, but had a difficult time finding land. They finally settled west of Albany. The Scotch-Irish, who had endured poverty as tenant farmers in Ireland, rejected New York for New Jersey, because they did not cross the ocean just to be tenants again.

By 1720 New York had about 36,000 colonists, and about one in five New Yorkers lived in New York City. Albany, with a port on the Hudson River, was New York's second largest town, with about 3,000 residents. The colony's population included more than 5,000 African Americans. Some New Yorkers used slaves as house servants, or put them to work in businesses or on fishing boats. Free blacks were forbidden from owning land or houses in New York.

The Blue Bell Tavern, a popular gathering place in colonial New York City. Colonial cities remained small by modern standards, and were mostly surrounded by fields and trees.

William Kidd, known to legend as Captain Kidd, was born in Scotland and went to sea as a young man. He was a privateer for England and operated against French ships. By 1690 Kidd had property in New York and sailed out of New York Harbor to protect the coast from enemy privateers. Kidd was believed to have turned to outright piracy off the coast of Africa around 1697, although some doubt the truth of this. Like many privateers, and even pirates, Kidd was welcome in high society. People were attracted by his dashing reputation and his wealth. He is shown here hosting a lavish party aboard his ship. When he returned to New York, he was arrested and sent to England for trial. Captain Kidd was found guilty and hanged in 1701. Some of his treasure was found near Long Island, and through the years, people have mounted treasure hunts, hoping to find more of it.

New York Harbor was a center of privateering. Like pirates, privateers attacked ships at sea to steal their cargo. Privateers, however, were licensed by the government to attack the ships of enemy nations during a war.

Sea captains had other ways of making money besides privateering and piracy. Some captains agreed to carry passengers who had no money, and sold them into indentured servitude when they arrived in the colonies. Servants were needed in the colonies to perform long hours of labor. Indentured servitude solved the problems of both master and servant. The master needed servants and the work they could do, and poor British people needed a way to pay for the voyage across the Atlantic. In 1732 a young woman sailed to America, hoping to be able to pay back the captain after she arrived. Instead, "In Nine Weeks from the time I left Ireland we arrived at New York …. The Captain got an Indenture wrote & Demanded of me to Sign it … threatening a Gaol [jail] if I refused … I therefore in a fright Signed, & … it Did well enough to Make me a Servant four Years. In Two Weeks time I was Sold."

5.
AT WAR WITH FRANCE AGAIN

As the British created colonies along the Atlantic Coast and slowly expanded westward, the French settled in Canada. Many French settlers lived like the Native Americans. They paddled their canoes westward in search of good land on which to hunt and trap. They returned to the settlements once a year to trade their furs for bullets, gunpowder, and other supplies. They followed the waterways through the wilderness all the way to the Mississippi River and along the Great Lakes into the upper midwest. Since they were the first Europeans to enter this region, they claimed it all for their country. The land became New France, a vast area stretching from the Allegheny Mountains to the Rocky Mountains and from Canada to Mexico.

For a long time British settlers did not move west of the Allegheny Mountains. But British trappers heard that the Ohio River Valley was rich in furs, so they began working west of the mountains. Naturally, French trappers did not like this. The French built a series of forts to block the British while encouraging the Native Americans to attack the British. The British government in turn ordered a fort to be built on the Ohio River, and told all the colonies to drive out any French trespassers.

Above: Benjamin Franklin designed this logo for the Albany Congress of 1754 in an effort to encourage the colonies to cooperate. The drive for union failed in 1754, but the snake reappeared in the years leading up to the Revolution.

Right: Albany was the site of an important meeting in 1754, attended by representatives from other British colonies. The town still had a lot of Dutch residents and retained a Dutch character.

In June 1754 representatives from seven colonies and the Iroquois League met in Albany to discuss cooperation against the French. The colonial representatives gave gifts to the Iroquois, hoping to win their support, but the Iroquois chose to wait and see which nation was most likely to win. The Albany Congress also discussed a bold plan for a union among the colonies, but in the end, the colonies feared that they would lose control over their own affairs, and the British government feared it would lose control over the colonies.

Meanwhile, the governor of Virginia had sent 21-year-old George Washington to the Ohio Valley to tell the French to withdraw. The French refused. Then, even as the Albany Congress met, the French drove away some Virginia militia who were building a fort at the place that

After the French and Indian War, the British government issued the Proclamation of 1763 forbidding colonists from settling west of the Allegheny Mountains. Many settlers ignored the Proclamation and angered the Iroquois.

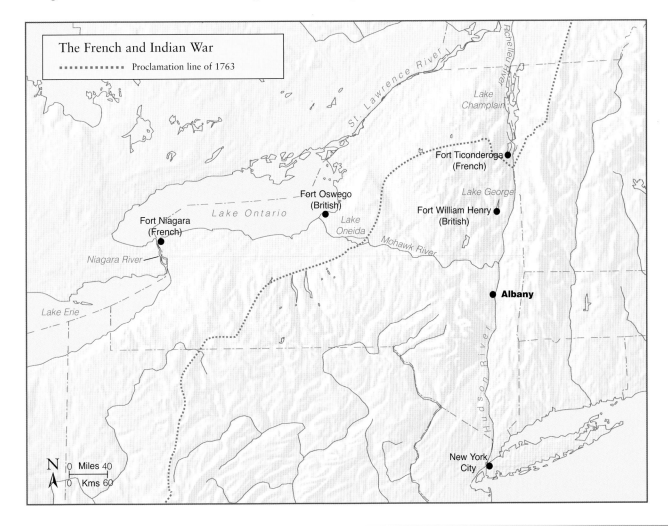

The French and Indian War

············· Proclamation line of 1763

became Pittsburgh, Pennsylvania. Washington and a small force returned to the area and attacked the French. On July 3, 1754, some 500 French and 400 Native Americans attacked and defeated Washington and his men. This series of small battles, fought to control the Ohio Valley, erupted into a European war between **Great Britain** and France. In North America, British settlers called it the French and Indian War. In Europe, people called it the Seven Years' War.

New York proved to be an important battleground in this war. Because few roads existed at this time, military operations followed along rivers and lakes. The traditional invasion route from Canada to New York went along the Richelieu River to Lake Champlain, Lake George, and the Hudson River. Between 1755 and 1760, French and British forces fought along this invasion corridor. They also fought along the Mohawk River Valley, and on the shores of Lake Ontario.

The French captured Fort Oswego in 1756, depriving New York of its most important frontier post. The following year a French and Native American force attacked Fort William Henry on Lake George and forced the British troops

GREAT BRITAIN: NATION FORMED BY ENGLAND, WALES, SCOTLAND, AND NORTHERN IRELAND; THE TERM "GREAT BRITAIN" CAME INTO USE WHEN ENGLAND AND SCOTLAND FORMALLY UNIFIED IN 1707.

The guns of Fort Ticonderoga, overlooking Lake Champlain. Fort Ticonderoga was built by the French in 1755.

stationed there to surrender. The Native Americans then violated the terms of the surrender and scalped, captured, or killed hundreds of the soldiers. To continue the war, New York and several other colonies together agreed to supply several thousand fighting men. The British army made a major effort in 1758 when it tried to storm Fort Ticonderoga on Lake Champlain. The British suffered a bad defeat, losing nearly two thousand killed and wounded.

The Six Nations of the Iroquois League had decided to avoid getting involved in the war between France and England. This policy of neutrality had worked well for the Iroquois in the past. However, the war caused division among the Six Nations. The Mohawks trusted the British Superintendent of Indian Affairs, William Johnson. In the past, Johnson had worked hard on behalf of the Mohawks. When war came, Johnson took command of a

Above: William Johnson

Left: Thoyanoguen, also called Chief Hendrick, was a sachem of the Mohawks. He and William Johnson were good friends. Hendrick was killed in a battle against the French in 1755.

Above: William Johnson meeting with the Mohawks. Johnson received a knighthood and a noble title for his success in recruiting the Native Americans and leading them in battle.

Right: A fighter with Rogers' Rangers, a British unit in the French and Indian War. In a dark and savage episode of revenge, in 1759 Major Robert Rogers and his famous Rangers marched on a Native American village on the St. Lawrence River, torched the village, and killed the people, mostly women and children, as they tried to escape the flames.

force of American militia. Many Mohawks, and some Oneidas, fought alongside Johnson and his men. Together, in 1759, they captured Fort Niagara from the French.

Meanwhile, other Mohawks who lived in New France sided with the French. Some of the Seneca and Cayuga people also helped the French. The Algonquian tribes of the Delawares and Mahicans sided with the French. All raided New York frontier settlements, and the land belonging to the Iroquois League became a battleground. British soldiers poured into Iroquois territory during the war, and settlers followed. Because the Iroquois League was divided during the war, it was less able to present a unified front after the war ended.

The year 1759 proved to be the decisive year of the French and Indian War. A British army landed near Quebec, the capital of New France. It fought and defeated a French army on the Plains of Abraham, just outside the

A log cabin in northern New York

A recreation of the interior of a 1700s New York log cabin

walls of Quebec. The British then captured Fort Ticonderoga and gained control of Lake Champlain.

By 1760 the British had completed the conquest of most of Canada. Fighting continued in Europe and at sea for two more years. In 1763 France and Great Britain made a peace treaty by which Canada became a British colony, just like the thirteen American colonies to the south. The victory ended the French threat to the thirteen colonies. It allowed Americans to move rapidly west onto land that had been controlled by the French and their Native American allies.

The British had promised the Iroquois that they would not occupy former French forts located in Iroquois territory. When the British broke their promise, many western Iroquois people and other western Native Americans took up arms against them, attacking frontier settlements from Virginia to New York. This conflict became known as Pontiac's Rebellion, lasting from 1763 to 1765. It further weakened the once mighty Iroquois League.

6.
REVOLUTION

The war with France had cost Great Britain a lot of money. Since British soldiers had been sent to America to help defend the colonists against the French Native Americans, British authorities thought that the colonists should help pay for the soldiers. The British **Parliament** imposed taxes on the colonists, enraging many of them. The first major new tax law was the Sugar **Act** of 1764. The act called for import and export duties, or taxes, to be paid on many trade goods, such as sugar, coffee, indigo, and animal hides. The British sent royal navy ships to patrol the American coast and enforce the law. They also assigned customs officials to collect the taxes and had merchants arrested who were thought to be evading the taxes.

Next, in 1765, Parliament passed the Stamp Act. Under the Stamp Act, colonists had to pay to have most documents stamped, or risk arrest. Even newspapers had

Above: Whaling ships sailed from ports on eastern Long Island and searched for whales around Newfoundland and Greenland. Colonists used the whale fat for lamp oil or candles.

Below: Sawmills churned out lumber, one of New York's major raw materials exports.

to have stamps. The Stamp Act affected colonists of all social classes, and resistance grew throughout the colonies. Groups calling themselves the Sons of Liberty attacked the offices and homes of tax collectors. Riots broke out throughout the colonies, including a riot in New York to protest the arrival of the tax stamps. Leaders from eight colonies met in New York City in October 1765. This meeting, called the Stamp Act Congress, issued a statement that Parliament had no right to tax the colonies.

Below: By 1763, New York City had about 16,000 people, a college, a lending library, and a theater.

The Stamp Act was so unpopular that Parliament repealed it in March 1766. Still, King George III insisted that Great Britain's Parliament had the right to make laws for the colonies and collect taxes. Britain passed a new set of laws taxing even more products, which angered more colonists.

Tensions continued to grow between colonists and British soldiers and officials. In New York, the assembly refused to provide money to supply the British soldiers stationed there. So in 1767 Parliament decided to make an example of New York and acted to suspend New York's assembly. The act did not take effect because the assembly gave in quickly and voted to provide for the British soldiers.

In New York and other colonies, the leaders of opposition to British laws formed Committees of Correspondence throughout the colonies. By writing letters, the Committees would keep one another informed and make plans for the colonies to cooperate. They also planned to spread news that would influence public opinion in favor of rebellion. The Committees got all the colonies except New Hampshire to **boycott** English merchandise. The boycott convinced the British to repeal most taxes by 1770, except for the tax on tea.

Then Parliament passed a law that gave one British tea seller, the struggling East India Company, special

Below, Right: A colonial New York ferry dock. Ferries were vital for travel to and from colonial New York City.

Stagecoaches such as the "Flying Machine" sped between New York and Philadelphia. The trip took two or three days, including overnight stops at taverns or inns in New Jersey.

treatment. The East India Company was given a monopoly in the colonies, so that it could sell its tea more cheaply than any other dealer. Once again, the Committees of Correspondence went to work, spreading news of the latest law and the coming East India Company tea shipments. The Sons of Liberty organized actions against the shipments.

The first such action, the famous Boston Tea Party, occurred in December 1773 with the dumping of a large tea shipment into Boston Harbor. Riders carried the news to other cities. Even before the Boston Tea Party, New Yorkers had threatened merchants who sold East India Company tea, so that the merchants were unwilling to accept tea from the ship that was about to arrive. The royal governor had planned to protect the ship, but news of the Boston Tea Party so excited New Yorkers that the governor ordered the ship to leave without unloading its cargo of tea.

Great Britain responded to the Boston Tea Party by passing the Boston Port Act, which closed the port of

Boston and placed Massachusetts under military rule. Boston **patriot** Paul Revere rode to New York with news of the Boston Port Act, and New Yorkers agreed that they would not try to take over Boston's shipping business. Many in the colonies began to argue that they would have to fight for independence from Great Britain. All the colonies except Georgia agreed to meet in Philadelphia in September 1774.

The First Continental Congress met in Philadelphia on September 5, 1774. The congress drew up a set of resolutions stating the rights of the colonies to self-government, and formed a Continental Association to boycott English trade goods and organize local governments. Finally, the delegates agreed to meet again in May 1775. Before that date arrived though, the first battle of the American Revolution had been fought in Lexington and Concord, Massachusetts, on April 19, 1775. News of that battle, carried by a fast rider, took four days to reach New York.

The Second Continental Congress met in May 1775 in Philadelphia. At the second congress, the delegates voted to raise a Continental Army, with George Washington as its commander-in-chief. Meanwhile, Ethan Allen of New England had taken matters into his own hands and organized a force of patriots to capture Fort Ticonderoga, on Lake Champlain in New York. Allen captured the fort without a fight on May 10, 1775. Some members of Congress thought the fort should be returned, but they were swayed by the argument that the fort was vital to the American cause.

A year later, the Continental Congress met again in Philadelphia to vote for independence. Of the 56 men who signed the Declaration of Independence on July 4, 1776, four of them were from New York. A few days later, New York patriots celebrated by pulling down a large statue of King George III. They used the metal from the statue to make bullet molds and bullets.

The British quickly acted to secure New York City as their center of operations for putting down the rebellion. The British forces

> PATRIOT: AMERICAN WHO WANTED THE COLONIES TO BE INDEPENDENT OF GREAT BRITAIN

New York patriots pulled down the statue of King George III in celebration of the signing of the Declaration of Independence.

inflicted a series of defeats on General Washington and his army beginning in August 1776. In September, a house fire spread and destroyed 493 buildings in the city. By November, Washington and his army were forced to retreat to New Jersey. The British held New York City for the remaining years of the war, and thousands of **loyalists** flocked to the city to make their homes there. During the Revolutionary War, an estimated 11,000 American prisoners of war died on British prison ships anchored in New York Harbor.

In spite of the British occupation of New York City in April 1777, New Yorkers meeting at Kingston approved their first constitution as an independent state. A few months later, America's fortunes turned at Saratoga, north of Albany. On October 17, 1777, the Americans defeated a force of more than 5,000 British troops. However, British troops did not leave New York City until November 25, 1783. They were the very last British troops to leave an American city at the end of the Revolution.

Above, Left: Four men from New York—William Floyd (pictured), Philip Livingston, Lewis Morris, and Francis Lewis—signed the Declaration of Independence . Francis Lewis paid the greatest price for daring to sign the document. British troops destroyed his home and arrested his wife. George Washington arranged to exchange her for a British prisoner of war, but being in prison ruined her health and she died a few years later.

Left: In 1762, the date of this meeting, New York City had a firefighting company, but fires remained a major hazard of colonial city life.

The Battle of Harlem in September 1776 led to George Washington's loss of New York City.

Below: British General John Burgoyne (in red jacket) surrenders by handing over his sword to General Horatio Gates at Saratoga.

EPILOGUE

New York became the eleventh American state on July 26, 1788. New York City served as the capital of the United States from 1785 until 1790, and George Washington's inauguration as president was held there. Albany became the state capital.

The Revolutionary War proved to be a catastrophe for the Six Nations of the Iroquois League. The League divided during the war, with the Oneidas fighting with the American rebels and the Mohawks fighting with the British. By the time the war ended, almost all of the Iroquois villages had been destroyed. European people tried to force the remaining Iroquois to give them their lands. The Iroquois found themselves having to live on increasingly smaller plots of reservation land surrounded by white settlements. Most of the Iroquois left. Today, the descendants of some Iroquois people still live in reservation communities in New York.

The modern-day state of New York has a population of about 18 million. More than 7 million people live in New

The Statue of Liberty in New York harbor has become a symbol of American freedom. Millions of immigrants have been greeted on their arrival to the United States by this figure, which was given to the city by the people of France.

The inauguration in New York of George Washington as the first president of the United States

York City, and another 8 million live in the communities surrounding the city. New York City is a major center of the nation's culture and business, as well as a port of entry for immigrants from foreign lands. About ten percent of New York's population was born outside the United States; three quarters of a million of the foreign-born people are Asian Americans. African American people make up 2.5 million of New York state's population.

In addition to New York City, smaller cities such as Buffalo, Rochester, and Syracuse have grown throughout the state. Only 15 percent of New York's population lives in rural areas of the state, and 1 percent of the state's working people work in agriculture. Apples and grapes are both major agricultural products. About 16 percent of the working population works in manufacturing, and two important manufacturing products are flour and photographic equipment.

More than half of New York is forested, and bears and wildcats still roam the woods in the remotest areas. Deer, rabbits, woodchucks, raccoons, porcupines, and beavers are abundant. Visitors enjoy the natural beauty of New York at such places as Niagara Falls, the Finger Lakes, and the Catskill Mountains.

Fort Ticonderoga, scene of battles during both the Revolution and the French and Indian War, has been reconstructed and is open to visitors. Saratoga National Historical Park preserves the Revolutionary War battlefield where the tide turned in the Americans' favor.

Saratoga National Historical Park. The American Revolution battle was not the first battle for this land. In the 1730s, white settlers began to move onto land near Saratoga, claiming they had a deed from the Mohawks. Mohawk leaders said there was no such deed. For nearly 30 years the Mohawks fought a legal battle for the land. Although in the end they were paid for the land, they never got the land itself back.

DATELINE

1570: Native American tribes form what will become known as the Iroquois League around this time. Five Native American tribes belong to the League by about 1600.

1609: Henry Hudson is the first European to sail up the Hudson River.

1611: Henry Hudson's sailors mutiny and set Hudson adrift in frigid northern waters.

1614: The Dutch East India Company builds a trading post, Fort Nassau on the Hudson River, at the site of modern-day Albany.

1621: Dutch merchants organize the Dutch West India Company.

1624: Dutch traders settle at Fort Orange on the Hudson River, near the site of the former Fort Nassau, establishing the Dutch colony of New Netherland.

1625: Dutch settlers found New Amsterdam on Manhattan Island.

1626: Dutch officials purchase Manhattan Island from the Delaware (Lenni-Lenape) people.

1646: Peter Stuyvesant becomes Director General of New Netherland.

1655: New Netherland takes over New Sweden, in present-day Delaware.

AUGUST 27, 1664: Stuyvesant surrenders New Netherland to the English, who rename the colony New York.

1673: The Dutch briefly recapture New York but return it to English control a year later.

1683: New York's first elected colonial assembly meets.

1701–1755: The Iroquois League enjoys a "golden age," a period of great power and prosperity.

1754: Representatives from seven colonies meet at Albany and discuss a plan of union.

1754–1760: Battles of the French and Indian War are fought from Pennsylvania to Canada, with many taking place in New York.

NOVEMBER 1776: British troops force George Washington's army out of New York, and occupy the city for the duration of the American Revolution.

APRIL 1777: New York approves a state constitution.

OCTOBER 17, 1777: Americans inflict a decisive defeat on the British at Saratoga.

MAY–NOVEMBER 1779: Ruthless American campaign destroys Iroquois towns, crops, and orchards. The Six Nations never recover.

NOVEMBER 25, 1783: The British army leaves New York City.

JULY 26, 1788: New York becomes the eleventh state in the United States.

Glossary

ACT: law, so called because it is made by an act of government

AMERICA: land that contains the continents of North America and South America

BOYCOTT: agreement to refuse to buy from or sell to certain businesses

BRITISH: nationality of a person born in Great Britain; people born in England are called "English"

CHARTER: document containing the rules for running an organization

COLONY: land owned and controlled by a distant nation; a colonist is a permanent settler of a colony

DUTCH: nationality of people born in the Netherlands

FRONTIER: newest place of settlement, located the farthest away from the center of population

GREAT BRITAIN: nation formed by England, Wales, Scotland, and Northern Ireland; the term "Great Britain" came into use when England and Scotland formally unified in 1707.

HOLLAND: main province of the Netherlands, often used incorrectly to refer to the Netherlands

INDENTURED SERVANT: person who agreed to work as a servant for a certain number of years in exchange for food, clothing, a place to sleep, and payment of one's passage across the Atlantic to the colonies

INDIANS: name given to all Native Americans at the time Europeans first came to America, because it was believed that America was actually a close neighbor of India

LONGHOUSE: long structure with a rounded roof, made of bent saplings covered with bark, and divided into rooms by partitions

LOYALIST: colonist who wanted America to remain a colony of Great Britain

MAHICAN / MOHEGAN / MOHICAN: three different ways of spelling the name of the Algonquian-speaking Hudson valley Native Americans who competed unsuccessfully for land and trade with their Mohawk rivals

MANOR: in England, an estate owned and governed by a lord, who had authority over the tenants who farmed the land; also, the lord's house on the estate

MERCHANT: trader; person who buys and re-sells merchandise

MILITIA: group of citizens not normally part of the army who join together to defend their land in an emergency

MONOPOLY: exclusive right to control the purchase and sale of specific goods or services

MUTINY: rebellion against authority, especially by soldiers or sailors

NATIVE AMERICANS: people who had been living in America for thousands of years at the time that the first Europeans arrived

NETHERLANDS: "low countries"; a European nation formed by the union of several low-lying provinces, including Holland. Amsterdam is the capital city.

NEW WORLD: western hemisphere of the earth, including North America, Central America, and South America; so-called because the people of the Old World, in the east, did not know about the existence of the Americas until the 1400s

OLD WORLD: Europe, Asia, and Africa

PARLIAMENT: legislature of Great Britain

PATRIOT: American who wanted the colonies to be independent of Great Britain

PATROON: Dutch word for "protector", a person who received manorial rights over a large estate in return for bringing colonists to New Netherland

PELT: skin and fur of an animal

PROTESTANT: member of any Christian church that has broken away from Roman Catholic or Eastern Orthodox control

PURITANS: Protestants who wanted the Church of England to practice a more "pure" form of Christianity, and established a colony in New England

SACHEM: Algonquian word for chief

TENANT: one who pays rent for farm land owned by a landlord

WAMPUM: Algonquian word for beads made of shells and used as money

FURTHER READING

Bial, Raymond. *The Iroquois*. New York: Marshall Cavendish, 1999.

Collier, Christopher, and James Lincoln Collier. *The French and Indian War, 1660–1763*. Tarrytown, N.Y.: Marshall Cavendish, 1998.

Russell, Francis. *The French and Indian Wars*. New York: American Heritage, 1962.

Smith, Carter, ed. *Battles in a New Land: A Source Book on Colonial America*. Brookfield, Conn.: Millbrook Press, 1991.

Smith, Carter, ed. *The Revolutionary War: A Source Book on Colonial America.* Brookfield, Conn.: Millbrook Press, 1991.

Wilbur, C. Keith. *The Woodland Indians.* Old Saybrook, Conn.: Globe Pequot Press, 1997.

Yue, Charlotte, and David Yue. *The Wigwam and the Longhouse.* Boston: Houghton Mifflin, 2000.

WEBSITES

www.americaslibrary.gov
Select "Jump back in time" for links to history activities.

www.nps.gov/fone/relsites.htm
find links to French & Indian War-related parks.

http://www.fortedwards.org/cwffa/cwffhome.htm
Explore frontier forts involved in the French and Indian War.

http://www.newnetherland.org
Examine the site of the New Netherland Museum, with virtual tours of New Netherland and the *Half Moon*

http://www.pbs.org/wnet/newyork/laic/
Play the "Learning Adventures in Citizenship" game.

BIBLIOGRAPHY

The American Heritage History of the Thirteen Colonies. New York: American Heritage, 1967.

Jameson, J. Franklin. *Narratives of New Netherland, 1609–1664.* New York: Charles Scribner's Sons, 1909.

Kammen, Michael. *Colonial New York: A History.* New York: Charles Scribner's Sons, 1975.

Middleton, Richard. *Colonial America: A History, 1607–1760.* Cambridge, Mass.: Blackwell, 1992.

Taylor, Alan. *American Colonies.* New York: Viking, 2001.